B.L. 3.2
A.R. Quiz# 197521
Pts. 0.5

Cambodia

by Adam Markovics

Consultant: Marjorie Faulstich Orellana, PhD
Professor of Urban Schooling
University of California, Los Angeles

BEARPORT
PUBLISHING

New York, New York

Credits

Cover, © Patrick Foto/Shutterstock and © Ralf Siemieniec/Shutterstock; TOC, © kajornyot wildlife photography/ Shutterstock; 4, © Photomontage/Shutterstock; 5L, © GuoZhongHua/Shutterstock; 5R, © Hadynyah/iStock; 7, © Akarat Phasura/Shutterstock; 8, © Luis Castañeda/AGE Fotostock; 9T, © Michael Nolan/robertharding/ Alamy; 9B, © takepicsforfun/iStock; 10, © joakimbkk/iStock; 11, © Mauro Ladu/Alamy; 12, © Kjersti Joergensen/ Shutterstock; 13 (T to B), © Martin Mecnarowski/Shutterstock, © LenSoMy/iStock, and © Riverrail/Dreamstime; 14, © Zzvet/iStock; 15, © Chalermphon Kumchai/Dreamstime; 16, © Bridgeman Images; 17T, © PreechaB/ Shutterstock; 17B, © Samrang Pring/Reuters/Newscom; 18L, © vivanvu/Shutterstock; 18–19, © Bertrand Gardel/ hemis/AGE Fotostock; 20, © Sean Sprague/Alamy; 21, © Tibor Bognar/Avalon/Newscom; 22T, © Kika Mika/ Shutterstock; 22B, © Fernan Archilla/Shutterstock; 23, © Donyanedomam/Dreamstime; 24–25, © Toby Williams/ Dreamstime; 25R, © Samrang Pring/Reuters/Newscom; 26, © Rawpixel/iStock; 27, © Steve Vidler/mauritius images GmbH/Alamy; 28, © Rawpixel/Shutterstock; 29, © Stéphane Lemaire/hemis/AGE Fotostock; 30T, © Oleg_ Mit/Shutterstock, © Andreylobachev/Dreamstime, and © Yaroslaff/Shutterstock; 30B, © MickyWiswedel/iStock; 31 (T to B), © Yoann Neb/Shutterstock, © Bou Kanika/Shutterstock, © Dmitry Polonskiy/Shutterstock, © PreechaB/ Shutterstock, and © Tonkinphotography/Shutterstock; 32, © Mitrofanov Alexander/Shutterstock.

Publisher: Kenn Goin
Senior Editor: Joyce Tavolacci
Creative Director: Spencer Brinker
Design: Debrah Kaiser
Photo Researcher: Thomas Persano

Library of Congress Cataloging-in-Publication Data

Names: Markovics, Adam, author.
Title: Cambodia / by Adam Markovics.
Description: New York, New York : Bearport Publishing, 2019. | Series:
   Countries we come from | Includes bibliographical references and index.
Identifiers: LCCN 2018009271 (print) | LCCN 2018010081 (ebook) |
   ISBN 9781684027361 (ebook) | ISBN 9781684026906 (library)
Subjects: LCSH: Cambodia—Juvenile literature.
Classification: LCC DS554.3 (ebook) | LCC DS554.3 .M375 2019 (print) |
   DDC 959.6—dc23
LC record available at https://lccn.loc.gov/2018009271

For more information, write to Bearport Publishing Company, Inc., 45 West 21st Street, Suite 3B, New York, New York 10010. Printed in the United States of America.

10 9 8 7 6 5 4 3 2 1

Contents

STUNNING

ANCIENT

Joyful

Cambodia is a country in Southeast Asia.

It's about the same size as the state of Missouri.

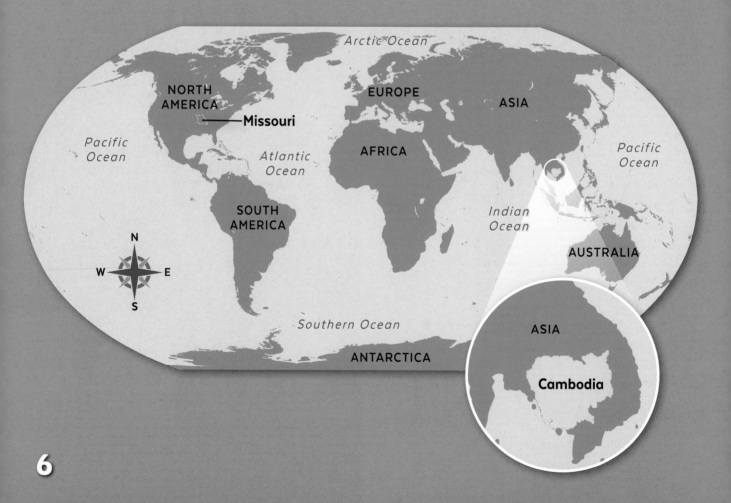

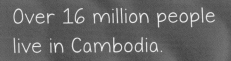

Over 16 million people live in Cambodia.

Much of Cambodia is covered by **plains**, forests, and rivers.

The Mekong River flows through the country.

People fish in its rich waters.

Tonle Sap is a huge lake in Cambodia. It's connected to the Mekong River.

9

Many Cambodians farm the plains.

They grow corn, tobacco, and lots of rice.

The rice is grown in special fields covered in water.

Farmers use buffalo to help plow the rice fields.

Wild animals live in Cambodia's forests.

Monkeys leap from tree to tree.

Leopards slink through **brush**.

Cobras slither across the ground.

Cambodia's forests are being cut down. People sell the wood for money. As a result, many animals are losing their homes.

Cambodia has a long history.
People settled there
thousands of
years ago.

From around
800 to 1400, the
Khmer (kuh-MAIR)
Empire ruled the land.

They built huge stone **temples**.

Angkor Wat is the most famous Khmer temple. It was built from millions of stone blocks!

Many years later, in 1863, France took control of Cambodia.

On November 9, 1953, the country became free.

In the 1970s, a **ruthless** group—the Khmer Rouge—took power.

They killed two million Cambodians.

victims of the Khmer Rouge

Today, a king rules Cambodia.

King Norodom Sihamoni

The **capital** of Cambodia is Phnom Penh.

It's also the country's largest city.

People zoom around in tuk-tuks.

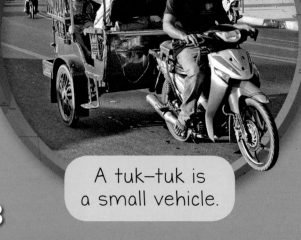

A tuk-tuk is a small vehicle.

Over 1.5 million people live in Phnom Penh.

19

Khmer is Cambodia's main language.

This is how you say *thank you* in Khmer:

Awkuhn (aw-KOON)

គុណា

This is how you say *water*:

Tuk (TUK)

ទឹក

Other languages spoken in Cambodia are Cham and French.

Cambodian food is full of flavor!

People enjoy grilled pork and rice.

pork

They slurp up spicy noodles.

Bugs are on the menu in Cambodia! People love to eat fried crickets and ants.

fried crickets

23

What sports are popular in Cambodia?

Kickboxing draws huge crowds.

Fighters kick each other with bare feet!

Buffalo racing is another popular sport.

Look around!

Many Cambodians wear colorful checkered fabric.

krama

It's called *krama*.

Krama can be worn as a hat, skirt, and in many other ways!

sampot

The *sampot* is a cloth worn around the lower body. It's often draped or folded and is worn by both men and women.

Cambodians love to perform.

Dancers curl their fingers and toes.

These movements tell a story!

leather puppets

Khmer shadow theater includes puppets made of leather.

Fast Facts

Capital city: Phnom Penh

Population of Cambodia: Over 16 million

Main languages: Khmer, Cham, and French

Money: Cambodian riel

Major religion: Buddhism

Neighboring countries: Laos, Thailand, and Vietnam

Cool Fact: Many Cambodians do not celebrate their birthday. Some older people do not even know their age!

Glossary

brush (BRUHSH) a thick growth of small trees, bushes, and shrubs

capital (KAP-uh-tuhl) a city where a country's government is based

plains (PLAYNZ) large, flat areas of land

ruthless (ROOTH-lis) very cruel

temples (TEM-puhlz) religious buildings where people worship

31

Index

Read More

Simmons, Walter. *Cambodia (Blastoff! Readers: Exploring Countries).* Minnetonka, MN: Bellwether (2012).

Yip, Dora. *Welcome to Cambodia (Welcome to My Country).* New York: Gareth Stevens (2001).

Learn More Online

To learn more about Cambodia, visit
www.bearportpublishing.com/CountriesWeComeFrom

About the Author

Adam Markovics lives in Ossining, New York. He has a pet rabbit named Pearl, who enjoys sitting next to him as he writes. He hopes to visit Southeast Asia with his wife one day soon.